H45 583 361 4

D1137389

'EARTH HAS NOT ANY THING
TO SHEW MORE FAIR'

*A View of the City of London, as it appears from under one of the
Arches of Westminster Bridge, published by R. Wilkinson, 58 Cornhill*

'Earth has not any thing to shew more fair'

A Bicentenary Celebration of Wordsworth's Sonnet
'Composed upon Westminster Bridge, 3 Sept. 1802'

Edited by Peter Oswald and Alice Oswald
and Robert Woof

with an essay by
Pamela Woof

SHAKESPEARE'S GLOBE &
THE WORDSWORTH TRUST
2002

Designed by Stephen Hebron
Typeset in 11/13 pt Adobe Bembo by The Wordsworth Trust
Printed in Great Britain on Munken Pure by Titus Wilson, Kendal

ISBN 1 870787 84 6

Contents

Foreword

Patrick Spottiswoode
Director, Globe Education

T HIS VOLUME WILL help to launch *Sonnets*, a project which aims to encourage students across the world to explore different sonnet forms by writing pentameters, couplets, quatrains and sestets about bridges in their communities.

While the Globe may not be in a position to commission as much new writing as the Globe of 1599, a commissioning tradition has been established. Sam Wanamaker, the Globe's Founder, commissioned poets to contribue to eleven volumes in the series "Poems for Shakespeare". Mark Rylance, the Globe's Artistic Director, commissioned Peter Oswald to write the first new play for the Globe, a verse drama entitled *Augustine's Oak*, for the 1999 Theatre Season. *The Golden Ass*, a second play for the Globe by Peter Oswald, was staged in 2002.

I turned to Peter for advice and help with *Sonnets*. He was immediately supportive of the idea of commissioning poets to contribute to a book and of establishing a series of writing workshops in schools. Alice and Peter Oswald agreed to select and approach poets to take part. I am indebted to them both for their encouragement and for helping to shape the content and scope of the *Sonnets* project as well as this book.

I was heartened by Robert and Pamela Woof's immediate offer of support, as the Wordsworth Trust is an ideal as well as an obvious partner. Robert agreed to prepare the volume for publication under the Wordsworth Trust's imprint and Pamela agreed to provide an introductory essay on the Wordsworth sonnet. They have both been exceptionally generous with their time and knowledge.

Alice, Peter, Pamela and Robert have also contributed to the second phase of the *Sonnets* project. Web resources, providing support for the workshops in schools, include recorded discussions led by Robert between several of the poets included in this volume. I am very grateful to Jerome Monahan for editing the *Sonnets* page and resources for the Globe website. Thanks to South Bank University for providing Globe Education with recording studios.

I would also like to thank the Trustees and Directors of Shakespeare's Globe, Peter Kyle, Mark Rylance and John Nicholls for their support and encouragement; my colleagues in Globe Education and in particular, Deborah Callan, Fiona Banks, Lynda Phelan and Sarah Allen; Jeanne Strickland and the Education Advisory Committee; Nick Robins, Heather Neill and the Publications Committee; Lady Rupert Nevill and Professor Stanley Wells.

However, this volume only exists because thirty-seven poets agreed to celebrate the two hundredth anniversary of Wordsworth's sonnet. I hope their poems will inspire young poets in schools as Wordsworth's sonnet has inspired them.

Preface

Robert Woof
Director, The Wordsworth Trust

THE GLOBE THEATRE, so distinguished for its passionate bringing alive of Shakespeare – and his contemporaries – so exciting in the way it has brought to audiences theatre as it was played when Shakespeare wrote and acted, has a concern too for the poetry that is not drama, for the poetry that is communication, meditation. The understanding of how poetry works both as the medium of theatre and as individual human utterance is essentially one thing; we are on the way to understanding a play if we understand the sonnet. Drama is played out in plays; we see it. In poems the drama is played in the reader's mind. But both depend on words, and Globe Theatre Education is to add to its remarkable achievement of celebrating words in drama by turning for a special occasion to mark words in poetry.

The occasion is the celebration, on 3 September 2002, of Wordsworth's great sonnet, 'Composed upon Westminster Bridge', with its famous opening, 'Earth has not any thing to shew more fair'. Wordsworth wrote this two hundred years ago, and the Wordsworth Trust, established in Grasmere, Cumbria, with Wordsworth's home, Dove Cottage, at its centre, has combined with Globe Education to launch a wide-ranging celebration of this composition. Perhaps the most important aspect of this celebration is a creative writing project in which many schools will participate. Sonnets by Shakespeare and Wordsworth particularly will be explored, and students from schools and colleges will be encouraged to write their own sonnets or poems in another form.

One important aspect of the project has been to invite thirty-seven British poets to reflect on Wordsworth's sonnet and to ask them to respond in the poetic form of their choice. Not surprisingly, variants of the sonnet form dominate in the considerable variety of response. The songs and sonnets of these twenty-first century poets are rich in diversity and range. Some poets catch an image of Wordsworth himself, perhaps as a master writer, or, again, as the political comforter, say, of the black leader, the West Indian, 'Toussaint L'Ouverture', imprisoned by Napoleon; another takes the bridge as an image of some haughty divinity, another as a metaphor for that very troubled human state of being 'mid-stream'; another celebrates the twenty-first century's view of London from the uplifted London Eye; and yet another sees the bridge as a place for the tourist whose child in the pram is the significant articulator of the grandeur; another regards it as a knowing place that sees through the posturing of politicians; and yet again, another as a very English place which might make a native Scot mindful of an equally heroic and perhaps preferred bridge in Scotland. Another poet sees the danger of optimistically claiming to be 'a bridge': a sort of naïve optimism leading to disaster for Czechoslovakia and its leaders. All the new poems are now published here together with an introductory commentary about how Wordsworth himself came to write his sonnet which expresses his surprised view of the city of London, as if it were not only seen under a new dawn but as the heavenly city itself.

Complementary to Pamela Woof's essay on Wordsworth's sonnet and to the various inventive responses of the poets, some of the poets have been invited to participate in discussions at the Globe about 'poetry and form', in general and the sonnet form in particular. These discussions have been recorded and edited by Jerome Monahan as part of a web resource for the participating schools, but they are not exclusively for those schools, for the resource will be available for all who are interested.

Both Globe Education and the Wordsworth Trust are committed to bringing the poetry of the past and the present together. Both institutions are committed to commissioning new writing – the Globe has commissioned two new plays as well as translations of three plays. The Wordsworth Trust is committed to writing residencies where the writer takes the themes of Romanticism and explores them freely, inventing the new, possibly discarding the past, but keeping the quick of the shaping spirit of the imagination. Wherever this programme of new writing takes place, it will be led by poets who will encourage both students and teachers to consider the relationship between form and content – to explore the world through pentameters, couplets, quatrains, octets and sestets. It may involve looking at poems of the seventeenth, nineteenth and twenty-first centuries, but in the end it is possible that the pleasures of form will set free the writers to confront new themes. Wordsworth said that he wrote 'on man, the heart of man, and human life', knowing as well as Shakespeare pre-eminently did, that writing was in defiance of Time. It was Wordsworth's strategy to offer his work to the young:

> I will relate the same
> For the delight of a few natural hearts;
> And, with yet fonder feeling, for the sake
> Of youthful Poets, who among these hills
> Will be my second self when I am gone.
> ('Michael', 35-39)

As a permanent mark of this celebration, the Wordsworth Trust, with other well-wishers of the poet and especially of his sonnet, have applied to place the text of Wordsworth's poem permanently on Westminster Bridge, and we are delighted that Westminster City Council have, in principle, given this their support. The proposed text has been set in the fine eighteenth-century typeface of John Baskerville, designed by David Esslemont, and executed by Cooper Engravers, Staveley. The event is indeed celebratory, and hopefully it will be accompanied by the gravitas and élan that the poets of today bring to the occasion.

Special thanks to Alice and Peter Oswald for facilitating the commissioning of the poems, to the poets themselves who have participated, to Pamela Woof for her introductory essay on Wordsworth's sonnet and to her and to Jerome Monahan who have joined me in devising the website discussions. John Fisher and Lynne McNab at the Guildhall Library, and John Sargent at the City of Westminster Archive Centre, were of great help in selecting the images. At the Wordsworth Trust, Sally Woodhead typed the essay and all the sonnets, David Cooper, Arts Officer, has helped edit the short biographies, and Stephen Hebron has designed this book.

I. *Wordsworth's Sonnet*

Opposite: Wordsworth's sonnet, as first published in volume one of *Poems in Two Volumes,* 1807

[Wordsworth did not correct the date to Sept. 3, 1802 until he published his collected sonnets in 1838.]

14.

COMPOSED UPON

WESTMINSTER BRIDGE,

Sept. 3, 1803.

Earth has not any thing to shew more fair:
Dull would he be of soul who could pass by
A sight so touching in it's majesty:
This City now doth like a garment wear
The beauty of the morning; silent, bare,
Ships, towers, domes, theatres, and temples lie
Open unto the fields, and to the sky;
All bright and glittering in the smokeless air.
Never did sun more beautifully steep
In his first splendor valley, rock, or hill;
Ne'er saw I, never felt, a calm so deep!
The river glideth at his own sweet will:
Dear God! the very houses seem asleep;
And all that mighty heart is lying still!

Left: William Wordsworth by Henry Edridge, 1806, and right: Dorothy Wordsworth by an unknown artist, c.1806

Westminster Bridge:
Dorothy and William Wordsworth

Pamela Woof

I

On Thursday morning, 29th, we arrived in London. Wm
left me at the Inn – I went to bed &c &c &c – After
various troubles & disasters we left London on Saturday
morning at ½ past 5 or 6, the 31st of July (I have forgot
which) we mounted the Dover Coach at Charing Cross.

(*The Grasmere and Alfoxden Journals*, World's Classics, 2002, p. 123)

IT WAS THE end of July 1802. Dorothy Wordsworth, aged
thirty, and her brother William, thirty-two, were on their way
to France, to Calais, to meet Annette Vallon and Annette's and
Wordsworth's daughter Caroline, born nine and a half years
before in Orléans. Prevented by war, Wordsworth had not seen
Annette since 1792 and had never seen Caroline.

The Wordsworths had come down from the Hutchinsons'
farm, Gallow Hill, Brompton, near Scarborough, Yorkshire,
where they had been for some ten days. Mary Hutchinson, an
old Penrith friend of Dorothy's (and of Wordsworth), was
keeping house with her sister Sara for their brother Tom at
Gallow Hill, and was to marry Wordsworth in the autumn.
The 1802 Peace of Amiens made it at last possible for the
English to visit France, and as far back as 22 March Dorothy
had written in her Journal, 'we resolved to see Annette'. Mary
agreed. Wordsworth and Dorothy met Annette in Calais, and

stayed for the month of August. Apart from talking with Annette and getting to know his child there might well be certain legal and financial arrangements to see to. We have no details;* Dorothy's Journal at this point is discreet, so discreet indeed about Wordsworth, Annette and Caroline that it was possible for a copy of the Calais section (*Grasmere and Alfoxden Journals*, pp. 124-5) to be made, probably for friends to read. This copy is torn and incomplete, and like the original it is far less about personalities than it is descriptive. Readers would learn little. They would read about 'delightful walks after the sun was set and the heat of the day passed', about the Evening star and the glory of the sky, about the distant lights of England and the near lights of boats upon the water; Annette and Caroline are referred to only once and then, by initials – 'we walked by the sea-shore every evening with A. and C; or William and I alone' – and the final mention of Caroline in the original, 'Caroline was delighted', is omitted. Dorothy seems more concerned with what had delighted Caroline, the 'streams of glowworm light', for in her copy she brings in that phrase an extra time and at an earlier point in her description:

* All we know is that Coleridge had been given to understand that Wordsworth and Dorothy would be back from Calais at least 2½ weeks before they actually did return: 'I wish, I wish they were back! – When I think of them in Lodgings at Calais … Dear little Caroline! – Will she be a ward of Annette? – Was the subject too delicate for a Letter? – I suppose so. – ' (from a letter to Sara Hutchinson, 10 August 1802). The mention of Caroline and the sentences about her – the only existing reference to Annette and Caroline in Coleridge's letters – have been heavily deleted. The subject clearly was too delicate for a letter, and it is not quite clear what it means. Again, Wordsworth would have little money at this point though he had known since mid-June that James Lowther's heir intended to pay financial claims arising from debts of the former Lord Lonsdale. Arrears of salary owing to the Wordsworths' father (with interest) would now be paid, but in any case war soon intervened to stop any transactions with France. After Waterloo, when Caroline married in 1816, Wordsworth did settle an annuity upon her.

Annette Vallon by an unknown artist

On calm hot nights we used to amuse ourselves with watching the motions of that glowworm light in the sea which added so much to the awful effect of the thunderstorm.

But the Calais adventure was yet to come. When Dorothy and her brother arrived in London on 29 July 1802 they were setting out; they were on their way. Mary had come some little distance with them from Gallow Hill and had been travel-sick 'from the smooth gliding of the Chaise', as was Dorothy; Wordsworth and Dorothy had slept for a few hours at Hull and the next night at Lincoln, had chosen not to dine at Peterborough but to walk instead round the outside of the Minster, and, travelling through the night, they had reached London on Thursday morning, 29th July. 'I went to bed &c &c

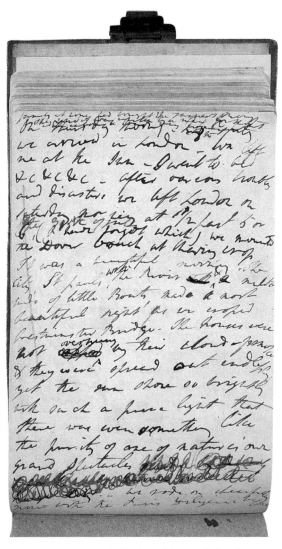

*A page from Dorothy Wordsworth's Journal, describing
the view from Westminster Bridge on 31 July 1802
(Wordsworth Trust, Dove Cottage, Grasmere)*

&c'. Dorothy says nothing about that Thursday (after some surely much needed rest) or about the whole of Friday in London. She does not enlarge upon '&c &c &c' or the 'troubles & disasters'. We have to remember that all this was written up later, when the drama of France and of Wordsworth's and Mary's wedding day was over. It was not until perhaps the third week in October, back in Grasmere, that Dorothy consulted her memory, and perhaps her notes, and wrote her account.

Her indifference and lack of detail in the sentences about London prior to the Wordsworths' mounting the Dover Coach (see the initial quotation above) is in telling contrast to the care and attention which she bestows upon the very next sentences describing the view from Westminster Bridge:

> It was a beautiful morning. The City, St pauls, with the River & a multitude of little Boats, made a most beautiful sight as we crossed Westminster Bridge. The houses were not overhung by their cloud of smoke & they were spread out endlessly, yet the sun shone so brightly with such a pure light that there was even something like the purity of one of nature's own grand Spectacles. We rode on chearfully ...

She made changes as she wrote: she had first written 'St pauls, the River with a multitude of little Boats ...', revising this to 'St pauls, with the River & a multitude ...'; she had originally had the houses as not 'capped' by their pall of smoke, and had changed 'capped' to the word 'overhung'. She discarded two lines completely, crossing them through in an emphatic and heavy manner: her phrase, 'like the purity of one of nature's own grand Spectacles', was originally followed by words immediately deleted which appear to read, 'made by herself & for herself thrown over that huge City.' And then, after this lingering over the view of London from high on the coach, within a single sentence we are at Dover. There is no further halting to weigh sentences and try them out. Even though Dorothy now goes back to mention the 'little plots of hop ground like vineyards' on the way to Dover, and notes that a woman on the top of the coach told her that it was a bad hop year and a 'sad thing for the poor people', there is very little slowing down to alter the manuscript, until this entire Calais section, itself a brief summary of the month in France, is almost at an end. Dorothy writes then at some leisure, amending and refining her prose, about the evening light over the sea and sands, the 'greenish fiery light' of waves breaking, and Caroline's delight in the 'sparkles balls shootings, & streams of glowworm light' in the wash of little boats at night.★

Why does Dorothy in such a summarising retrospective account give so much attention to the view from Westminster Bridge? Certainly at half past five or six in the morning '(I have forgot which)' it 'made a most beautiful sight', and Wordsworth clearly thought so too,

Earth has not any thing to shew more fair.

★ It is likewise in the evening light that Wordsworth places his own single and oblique reference to Caroline during this August in Calais. The octet of his sonnet, 'It is a beauteous Evening, calm and free', is entirely a presentation of two elemental forces: that of light from a setting sun, 'The gentleness of heaven is on the Sea'; and simultaneously that of the Sea's 'sound like thunder', the sound of the Sea as a 'mighty Being' with his 'eternal motion'. Not until the sestet do we fully realise that it is in this powerful and protective context of permanence and holiness that the poet is addressing a particular person:

Dear Child! dear Girl! that walkest with me here …

The reference is entirely discreet, but not the less loving.

*View of London from new Charing Cross, showing smoke
rising from the South Bank, c.1800, signed 'Roberts'.*

Both writers noted the lack of the usual smoke and the purity
of the light; both claimed that the beauty was comparable
with that in the natural world; Wordsworth used, and Dorothy
perhaps tried out, the notion that such unexpected and pure
beauty in the City was as a garment that the City might be
wearing – in Dorothy's abandoned words, 'made by herself &
for herself thrown over that huge City'. It was perhaps as a
result of discarding this complicated clothing image that she
changed 'capped' to 'overhung'. There are no 'Ships, towers,
domes, theatres and temples', except that St Paul's is named, in
Dorothy's impressionistic sketch; she picks out the 'houses',
ordinary domestic dwellings, and these are 'spread out end-
lessly'. There are no ships in her account; she recalls 'a multitude of little Boats'. In her City people live everyday lives.

Dorothy's sketch is no more than that, a sketch in a
written-up Journal, far distant from Wordsworth's finished
sonnet. Yet some of the same ideas are in both accounts. Is

*View of Westminster Bridge, showing he height of the parapet,
by an unknown artist, published June 1792 by T. Malton.*

Wordsworth's sonnet taking Dorothy's thoughts and expand-
ing them? Is Dorothy alluding to the sonnet in her retrospective account? Dates provided by Wordsworth are of no
help. He told Isabella Fenwick in the 1840s that the sonnet
was 'Composed on the roof of a coach, on my way to France,
Sepbr. 1802'. As we know, it was 31 July, not some time in
September, that he was on his way to France. Returning, he
and Dorothy drove back over Westminster Bridge, again at six
in the morning, and into London on 31 August. They had
'mounted the coach at ½ past 4' the previous afternoon in
Dover and had driven all night. But, on 31 August 'It was
misty & we could see nothing', wrote Dorothy. Another
London dawn; this time an unremarkable crossing of the
Bridge. When Wordsworth published the sonnet in his collection, *Poems in Two Volumes*, 1807, he gave it the heading,
'Composed upon Westminster Bridge, Sept. 3, 1803' and the

poem remained inexplicably under this date until Wordsworth collected his near 500 sonnets (to date) in one volume in 1838. The sonnet's date then became 'Sept. 3, 1802'.

We must suppose that on that glorious morning of 31 July 1802, Wordsworth and Dorothy, sitting on the roof of the Dover coach, talked to each other, exclaimed at the magnificent sight, the stillness and lack of smoke, thought of the City as wearing a beautiful garment, as having 'even something like the purity of one of nature's own grand Spectacles.' They 'rode on chearfully', but the seeds of the poem were sown most likely in a coach-top conversation, and elements and images from this would remain memorable because of shared talk. Traces of such shared talk are evident again and again in the Journal – talk about a leech-gatherer, about chasing butterflies as children, about daffodils by Ullswater (see *The Wordsworths and the Daffodils*, Wordsworth Trust 2002), about the shape of the umbrella yew-tree, about the moon on a particular night, about poems – his own or another's, Ben Jonson's or Spenser's or Coleridge's, about glow-worms, about birds, about what their neighbour Aggie Fisher said or, another neighbour Peggy Ashburner, about the manners of the rich, about night-skies, about anything. Without directly giving us the conversations, in the manner of Boswell recording Dr Johnson, the Journal tells us of the constant communication that was the essence of Dorothy's relationship with her brother. Here, on top of a coach going over Westminster Bridge, the same images would feed both Dorothy's care over detail in the Westminster section of her retrospective account, and would lie seminal in Wordsworth's mind.

There is no existing working draft manuscript of 'Composed upon Westminster Bridge'. The only emendation we know is in the fair copy prepared in 1806-7 by Mary, Dorothy, and Sara Hutchinson, for Longman, the printer of the 1807 *Poems*. Here, either as a happy revision, or merely because of a copying error, the word 'soul' replaces, in Wordsworth's hand, the deleted word 'heart':

Dull would he be of soul...

Wordsworth composed a good deal in his head, and out of doors; a sonnet could be pretty well finished before it was committed to paper at all. He composed and assigned several sonnets to his 1802 August in Calais, and one can see how the sands at Calais would provide him with a perfect composing space. Hazlitt later recalled the contrasting walking and composing habits of Coleridge and Wordsworth:

> Coleridge has told me that he himself liked to compose in walking over uneven ground, or breaking through the straggling branches of a copsewood; whereas Wordsworth always wrote (if he could) walking up and down a strait gravel-walk, or in some spot where the continuity of his verse met with no collateral interruption.
>
> (*My First Acquaintance with Poets*, 1823)

There would be little 'collateral interruption' on the beach. The 'Westminster Bridge' sonnet was perhaps not written down as finished until 3 September, the date Wordsworth chose to keep as part of the title. He and Dorothy were then back in London. Coleridge must have liked the poem. Shortly before his 'going to Malta for his health', as Farington phrased it, he read on 25 March 1804 to an assembled company at Sir George Beaumont's in London 'some lines' by Wordsworth, 'lines upon Westminster Bridge & the scenery from it' (from *The Diary of Joseph Farington*, Yale 1978-1998).

The 'lines' were this sonnet. The sonnet was a form much in favour with Wordsworth during that 1802 August in Calais, and during the London September. He had been drawn to the

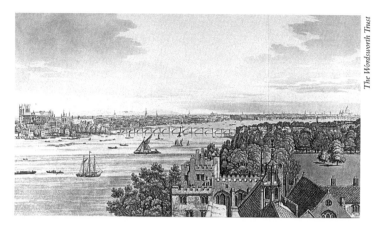

Joseph Farington's View of Westminster Bridge from Lambeth,
engraved by J. Stadler, 1795

sonnet since the afternoon of 21 May in Grasmere. 'Wm
wrote two sonnets on Buonaparte after', Dorothy recorded in
her Journal, 'I had read Milton's sonnets to him'. Recalling
that reading nearly forty years later Wordsworth told Miss
Fenwick that he had been

> … particularly struck on that occasion with the dignified
> simplicity and majestic harmony that runs through most
> of them [Milton's sonnets] … I took fire, if I may be
> allowed to say so, and produced three sonnets the same
> afternoon, the first I ever wrote, except an irregular one
> at School …

Wordsworth is inaccurate here about his own prior lack of experience in sonnet-writing – he had written several sonnets,
and had already published in *The Morning Post* his translation
of a sonnet from Petrarch and an original sonnet, but he is
quite accurate in his recollection that it was Milton who in
1802 newly inspired him. One of that afternoon's sonnets on

Buonaparte (the only one identified as composed on 21 May),
'I griev'd for Buonaparte', is, like perhaps half of Milton's, on
a theme of national interest.

Milton wrote fewer than twenty sonnets in English, 'Soul-
animating strains – alas, too few!', lamented Wordsworth
('Scorn not the Sonnet'). But if, on national and political
issues the 'Thing', in Wordsworth's words, 'became a Trumpet'
in Milton's hands, Milton could also use the sonnet to invite
a friend to an evening of wine and music, or to explore sub-
jects close to himself – his blindness, or his grief at his wife's
death, for example. This showed Wordsworth the way; he too
could range, even then in 1802 as he really took up the sonnet:
he could castigate the nation,

> The world is too much with us; late and soon,
> Getting and spending we lay waste our powers ...

or, sleepless, at a less profound and quite personal level, he
could count over

> A flock of sheep that leisurely pass by,
> One after one ...

entreating the refreshment of sleep; or, as in the 'Westminster
Bridge' sonnet, he could find himself for the first time on
Westminster Bridge in the light of a brilliant dawn and compose upon that chance subject, giving a sense of immediacy to
a sonnet as brilliant as the scene itself.

When providing advice in November 1802 for his sailor
brother John as to poetry to have by him on his next long
voyage, after suggesting Spenser, Wordsworth particularly
recommended Milton's sonnets, not only for their 'simplicity
and unity of object', but for their music, which has,
Wordsworth wrote,

... an energetic and varied flow of sound crowding into narrow room more of the combined effect of rhyme and blank verse than can be done by any other kind of verse I know of.

(from a fragment of a letter, dated Nov 1802)

That 'crowding into narrow room' was a stimulant to Wordsworth; he had written the long blank verse 'Ruined Cottage', the long stanzaic 'Peter Bell', a blank verse play, *The Borderers*, the free meditative paragraphs of both 'Tintern Abbey' and the great passages about his boyhood that would become part of *The Prelude*. He had succeeded, particularly in these blank verse poems, in finding a verbal music that could be sustained over an entire paragraph, with the syntax of the sentences falling over the line-endings and mounting into a rhythm that accorded with the singleness of thought that was often the basis of the paragraph. Narrative itself could be despatched quickly:

> With trembling hands I turned,
> And through the silent water stole my way
> Back to the Cavern of the Willow tree.
>
> (*Prelude*, 1805, I, 412-14)

But after this, a sentence of thirteen lines is needed to evoke the 'dim and undetermined sense / Of unknown modes of being' that by day and night invaded the mind of the boy who had 'stolen' the boat. Wordsworth, in other words, was ready for the sonnet; he could turn to the demands of the smaller form. Like the bees of his 1802 sonnet, 'Nuns fret not at their Convent's narrow room', bees that could

> soar for bloom,
> High as the highest Peak of Furness Fells ...

☞ LXXIII.

That time of year you may'ſt in me behold
When yellow leaves, or none, or few do hang
Upon thoſe boughs which ſhake againſt the cold,
Bare ruin'd choirs, where late the ſweet birds
In me thou feeſt the twilight of ſuch day, [ſang.
As after ſun-ſet fadeth in the weſt,
Which by and by black night doth take away,
Death's ſecond ſelf, that ſeals up all in reſt.
In me thou feeſt the glowing of ſuch fire,
That on the aſhes of his youth doth lie,
As the death-bed whereon it muſt expire,
Confum'd with that which it was nouriſh'd by.
This thou perceiv'ſt, which makes thy love more
ſtrong,   [long.
To love that well which thou muſt leave e'er

LXXIV.

But be contented : when that fell arreſt
Without all bail ſhall carry me away,

Thy ſ
Thy ·
The
And ·
The ·
Of m
Thou
Time
Look
Comr
Thoſe
To ta
Th
Sha

So oft
And f
As ev

A copy of Shakespeare's Sonnet 73 (with 'thou' inexplicably printed as 'you' in line 1) from vol. II of Wordsworth's own copy of The Works of the British Poets, *ed. Robert Anderson, 13 vols. 1795. Coleridge has placed marks of approval by some of the sonnets; the mark here indicates that Sonnet 73, though not of the supreme fourth class, is three classes higher 'in manner or style', than a sonnet of the 'first class of goodness ... all according to the feelings & taste of S.T.C.'.*

Wordsworth, from childhood, had a familiarity with Shakespeare. We find him in February 1835, writing to his old friend Wrangham and misremembering Sonnet 73:

I cannot forget that Shakepear, who scarcely survived 50 – (I am now near the close of my 65th year) wrote
          In me that time of life thou dost behold
          When yellow leaves, or few or none, do hang
          Upon the bough.

He remembered the rhythm, but clearly had no qualms about accuracy. He had long been aware of the 'felicitous feelings exquisitely expressed' of the Sonnets, and had deplored in 1815 their omission from recent editions of Shakespeare's works. Yet he had been, he remarked in 1836, 'almost habitually silent' upon the subject of Shakespeare: 'Who thinks it necessary to praise the sun?'

he could now leave the wide-ranging spaces of blank verse and 'murmur by the hour in Foxglove bells'. He could write sonnets. The compression of the form probably encouraged some other of Wordsworth's strengths: the ability to compose fine phrases, fine single lines, whole poems where every word must count; he could assume indeed the high rhetorical voice of public poetry:

We must be free or die, who speak the tongue
That Shakespeare spake.
('It is not to be thought of that the Flood / Of British freedom')

The freedom of subject-matter that the sonnet offered went hand in hand with constraints of form that involved more than the 'combined effect of rhyme and blank verse' which Wordsworth found so well managed in Milton. The structure itself was a challenge. With his own mastery of the blank verse paragraph behind him, Wordsworth again found himself following Milton. Milton had not used the Shakespearean sonnet of three separately rhyming verses of four lines each, with a concluding rhyming couplet (abab cdcd efef gg). That Shakespearean form could lend itself wonderfully, in Shakespeare's hands, to poems of image upon image – the declining time of year, the cold, the yellow leaves, summer birdsong silenced, tree branches, bare ruin'd choirs, twilight, sunset, night, sleep, death, a glowing fire, ashes, youth, life like fire feeding upon itself and drawing to the inexorable death-bed; and in the couplet, love ever stronger despite, almost because of, its mortal context. In such a sonnet (the example alluded to here is Shakespeare's sonnet 73) the quatrains, or 4-line verses, climb one upon the other, establishing from a single idea an emphatic and an ever-darkening pattern.

The Miltonic sonnet more frequently had to achieve its unity out of an opposition of ideas, out of a forceful dialogue within itself: Milton's passionate 'When I consider how my light is spent' with its octet complaint to God about the injustice of his becoming blind,

> Doth God exact day-labour, light deny'd,
> I fondly ask

is answered in the longer than usual sestet with a calm and calming statement about God's perfect serenity in the rightness of the diverse lots that fall to men:

> They also serve who only stand and wait.

Milton based his sonnet on the Italian model, often called Petrarchan. He was not the first to use this form; Sidney and Spenser in the last years of Queen Elizabeth I, in the 1580s and 1590s, had famously written sequences of courtly love poems to an almost unattainable mistress, as Petrarch had written to Laura. Milton freed the sonnet from this subject matter and from the need for sequence. He wrote sonnets as single poems, as did Wordsworth in 1802; though later, sonnet sequences were to become for Wordsworth alternatives to long poems of poetic contemplation.★

The Miltonic sonnet is unlike the Shakespearean in rhyming, as well as in its more oppositional form; Milton has generally eight lines using only two interlocking rhymes followed by six lines making use of a further two or sometimes three rhyming line-endings (abba abba cdcdcd, or, in the sestet, any other variant of two or three rhymes). Wordsworth

★Coleridge was soon to regret Wordsworth's 'habit' of writing 'such a multitude of small Poems'; he felt, in a way not entirely sympathetic to Wordsworth's inclination, that Wordsworth's 'natural Element' was the long philosophical poem, the projected *Recluse*, 'a Great Work, in which he will sail; on an open Ocean …' (from a letter to Thomas Poole, 14 October 1803).

chose the Miltonic constraint of having only four or possibly five rhymes to play with in his fourteen lines as against the Shakespearean greater ease of seven. Within this tight framework of eight lines and six, an octet and a sestet, Milton, to Wordsworth's admiration, did not always submit to a corresponding strict division of the sense into two parts:

> In the better half of his sonnets, the sense does not close with the rhyme at the eighth line, but overflows into the second portion of the metre. Now it has struck me, that this is not done merely to gratify the ear by variety and freedom of sound, but also to aid in giving that pervading sense of intense Unity in which the excellence of the Sonnet has always seemed to me mainly to consist.
>
> (from a letter to Alexander Dyce, 22 April 1833)

Wordsworth had written many sonnets when he thus came to consider the sonnet's construction. He went on in the same letter to complicate the two-part structure by placing it in tension with a three-part structure of thought: a sonnet 'ought to have a beginning, a middle, and an end … like the three propositions of a syllogism.' Indeed, it became less than useful for Wordsworth to think of the 'architecture' of the sonnet:

> I have been much in the habit of preferring the image of an orbicular body, − a sphere − or a dew-drop.
>
> (*ibid.*)

It would seem that within the brief, fourteen-line tight form of the sonnet, and conscious of both its two-part and three-part structure, what Wordsworth tried to achieve was what he had admired in the best of Milton's sonnets since 1802, 'simplicity and unity of object and aim'. His astonishing image for this in 1833, 'an orbicular body', evokes all that

Wordsworth might aspire to for the sonnet: that it should be like 'a sphere', a perfect mathematical shape, formal, intellectual and technically coherent; 'or a dew-drop', a clear form not quite perfectly spherical, a natural form that appears and disappears without man's calculation, that comes and goes of itself; for the sonnet, as Wordsworth conceived it, had to have the intellectual control of shape that the sphere evinces, and it had also to have at its best the clarity, naturalness and spontaneity of a dew-drop that had the freedom to be not entirely spherical, to offer a hint of a form that might be asymmetrical, and to be natural, a cry from the heart, an expression of feeling.

II

'Composed upon Westminster Bridge' is such a sonnet. Wordsworth represents the sonnet's speaker as being utterly stopped in his tracks by the unexpected beauty and forced to cry out his pleasure in a single line of absolute statement:

Earth has not any thing to shew more fair.

The whole poem from one aspect is an expansion of this line. What after all had Wordsworth's previous experience of London been – and he had lived in London for months as a young man – it had been, as he recalls in 1804-5,

the quick dance
Of colours, lights and forms, the Babel din
The endless stream of men, and moving things,
From hour to hour the illimitable walk
Still among streets …

Here, there, and everywhere, a weary throng,
The Comers and the Goers face to face,
Face after face ...

                    (*Prelude*, 1805, VII, 156–73)

'I had not thought death had undone so many', was to be the
way of putting it of a later poet; the 'endless stream of men' of
The Prelude, and the crowd that 'flowed over London Bridge'
of Eliot's *Waste Land* – both speak of the individual lost in a
river of humanity. And so, for Wordsworth on the last day of
July in 1802 the shock of stillness and beauty where only
meaningless weary movement had been known, produced
that breath-taking praise at his sonnet's opening. He could not
have begun more powerfully: the weight on that first syllable
is total, 'Earth'; not 'The World', which is both weaker in
sound and less elemental, but 'Earth', and the poem continues
as though expression rises unbidden. The sonnet is not presented as 'emotion recollected in tranquillity' but with all the
exclamation of present wonder.

   The second line is monosyllabic and equally weighty, its
normal word-order transposed so that full weight can fall
again on the first syllable, 'Dull':

   Dull would he be of soul who could pass by

It is the soul that will be quickened, the soul that will gain
from new insight. The eyes certainly register the surface
appearance – the City with its ships, towers, domes, theatres,
temples and houses; and the inner eye, for comparison, conjures up the valleys and hills of an absent natural beauty. But
the soul, by the end of the sonnet, will be nourished beyond
the intellect's pleasure in the neat City-country contrast and
identification that fits so well into the two-part structure of
octet and sestet, beyond the simultaneous satisfaction in the

three-part structure of beginning, middle and end, where the last lines, as in a syllogism, bring both parts together and seem to unite City and country in a trance-like calm.

The reader naturally sees himself as not dull of soul and is invited by the poem to ponder, to linger, not to 'pass by'. Wordsworth himself of course was 'passing by'; he was on the clattering Dover coach, crossing the bridge, and this would scarcely allow calm for thought, but the poem, composed perhaps on the beach at Calais, is composition, harmonious thought. It is not primarily a description of the scene – Dorothy's passage in the Journal is closer to that – Wordsworth's is 'composed' upon the scene. Further, to the title, that itself implies reflection, 'Composed upon Westminster Bridge', Wordsworth has added a most precise date, 'Sept. 3, 1803' – and it scarcely matters whether this is literally accurate or not. It is specific. These two parts in the title, the sense of composition and the precise date, prepare the reader, even before setting out into the sonnet, for that combination that is everywhere in Wordsworth: the presence of the real as the basis for the exaltation of thought.

Wordsworth had more than once before prevented his reader from 'passing by'. He had done it crudely enough in his first poem in *Lyrical Ballads*, 1798, 'Nay, Traveller! rest... .Who he was / That piled these stones ... I well remember' ('Lines left upon a Seat in a Yew-tree'), and then poet and reader together meditate upon the man's history; in 'Michael' (1800) Wordsworth had drawn to the reader's attention an

> object which you might pass by,
> Might see and notice not ...

and then, upon a heap of unhewn stones a life and meditation is based. Only extreme dullness of soul would allow anyone to pass by the Westminster Bridge sight because it was 'so touching in its majesty'. We have no intimation until line 5 as to what sight exactly could both touch the feelings and retain majesty. Majesty evokes power, admiration, awe, fear, impatience, contempt, but rarely pathos, compassion or feelings to touch the heart. We understand as we approach the end of the octet. The majesty is temporary; even as we see it we mourn its passing. Only like a garment that is no part of the real body, a garment providing perhaps an illusion, even a falseness, does the City wear the beauty of the morning. As we become aware in line 5 of that dawn light, we feel for the City and its unsustainable majesty, for mornings will change into the full light of day and London will waken to resume its accustomed and less appealing confusions.

Wordsworth hints at this through the adjective 'touching', through the emphasis on 'now': 'This City now doth like a garment wear the beauty ...' and, of course, through the garment image itself, but he will not let a notion of the impermanent darken too much the purity of the scene. His City is generalised, almost visionary; there is nothing specific, no 'St Paul's', no particular ships or buildings. We are given emblems of civilisation that could evoke any great city. And under the dawn light there is no action, no imperfection in these ships and buildings; they 'lie / Open unto the fields, and to the sky'. Fields, mainly on the southern banks of the Thames would be visible in 1802 from Westminster Bridge, as would an expanse of sky, and of course the river itself. Civilisation at its best would appear to be nestled in the natural world. The things of man, like individual man, would always be better, in Wordsworth's terms, for having space to 'lie / Open unto the fields and to the sky'. As individuals, Wordsworth had written in 1798,

> we can feed this mind of ours,
> In a wise passiveness.
>
> ('Expostulation and Reply')

*View south from the terrace of Somerset House towards Lambeth,
with the Surrey hills in the background, by William Daniell, 1805.*

We can 'lie Open unto the fields …'. There might be the same
calm for man living in close crowded groups, for man in cities,
could the elemental silence and exposure to sky and to the
natural world prevail. But it cannot. Already the word 'glittering' in line 8 carries a sense of surface sparkle that faintly
undermines the brightness, and the word 'smokeless' immediately conjures up the smoke that soon will disfigure the clear
buildings.

But the purity of the unreal City, for the moment, silent,
bare and unpeopled, is the dominant perception of the octet,
and Wordsworth's long cumulative sentence striding over line-
endings carries a conviction of the truth of the City's genuine
beauty. Even as we know that the City is simply wearing its
brightness as a temporary covering garment we accept with
equal belief that what the poet asks us to see as beautiful is
indeed beautiful. The ships, towers, domes are silent and bare
under a brilliant light. They are naked, exposed, fully known.
Certainly, they are ideal, but for once, here, the ideal is real; the

[26]

visionary is actual. The word 'bare' immediately following the garment comparison still worries literal readers and did worry people in Wordsworth's own day: 'Dear Mrs Kenyon was right', wrote Wordsworth to John Kenyon in September 1836,

as to the *bare* – the contradiction is in the *words* only – bare, as not being covered with smoke or vapour; clothed, as being attired in the beams of the morning. Tell me if you approve of the following alteration, which is the best I can do for the amendment of the fault.
The city now doth on her forehead wear
The glorious crown of morning; silent, bare,
Ships, towers, etc... .

How much richer it is to hold the apparent contradiction, and to find simultaneously its deeper offer of a glimpse, on a particular day in 1802 in London, of a timeless and ultimate City. Wordsworth never adopted his proposed amendment.

The pathos, the knowledge of time in the poem, is perhaps connected with the frail chance of history. Wordsworth never sought intimations of a world outside time; they were given, but he recognised them; they might flash again and again into the mind, as those chance-seen daffodils did, bringing with them a sense of joy at the perceived harmony, permanent order and patterning of creation seen alike in the stars in heaven and the flowers of earth. Or, as here, an occasion of travel might lead to a glimpse of what an eternal City could be like, a perfect City in an unfallen world, a vision. It is as though that morning, dated 3 September, was the first created morning, with the sun 'In his first splendor'. A pervasive dignity of language is conducive to such a grandeur of conception. The older form of two of the verbs, 'doth ... wear', 'glideth'; the preposition 'unto'; the emphatic inversions, 'Never did sun ...', 'Ne'er saw I, never felt'; the phrase 'at his own sweet will' with its Shakespearean echoes of sonnet 16's 'by your own sweet skill' or the 'sweet will' of sonnet 135; the apostrophe 'Dear God!' – all these evoke an earlier age, contribute to something even of a biblical tone, as indeed does the very subject of morning and purity. The Psalmist can address his Lord 'who coverest thyself with light as with a garment' (*Psalm* 104); it is in the morning that 'ye shall see the glory of the Lord' (*Exodus* 16); God will be there 'if I take the wings of the morning' (*Psalm* 139); his 'light shall break forth as the morning' (*Isaiah* 58); 'he shall be as the light of the morning when the sun riseth, even a morning without clouds' (2 *Samuel* 23); we are entreated to 'worship the Lord in the beauty of holiness' (*Psalm* 29). In just over a year Wordsworth, writing his autobiographical poem, will recall another morning, a magnificent morning, 'More glorious than I ever had beheld', when, as a youth, walking as it happened home along the fields in the Lake District after a country dance, he had felt a presence that was at once natural and spiritual:

> Ah! need I say, dear Friend, that to the brim
> My heart was full? I made no vows, but vows
> Were then made for me; bond unknown to me
> Was given, that I should be, else sinning greatly,
> A dedicated Spirit. On I walked
> In blessedness ...
>
> (*Prelude*, 1805, IV, 340-5)

The 'dear Friend' was of course Coleridge to whom *The Prelude* was addressed.

As Wordsworth moves from the octet of the 'Westminster Bridge' sonnet something of a similar blessedness is carried into the sestet, and the City's beauty is not diminished by the

wonder of morning as it appears in the best scenes Wordsworth knows, the hills and valleys of the natural world:

> Never did sun more beautifully steep*
> In his first splendor valley, rock, or hill;
> Ne'er saw I, never felt, a calm so deep!

Wordsworth is emphatic here: three times, with the word
'never' he elevates the beauty of the cityscape and the deep
calm of its effect, as being not only comparable to the fair
scenes referred to in line 1, but as being yet more profound
and paradisal. The calm penetrates the whole perceiving being
for Wordsworth: it is seen with the sensual eyes as though 'a
calm' is something tangible, and it is felt deep within, in the
inner self.

Along with this calm there is a complex of movements
underlying the sonnet: first of all, there is the Bridge itself, the
physical way to begin crossings: between North London and

---

*The word 'steep' used here and rarely for Wordsworth as a verb, must
undoubtedly have had one strong association for him; such a deep drench-
ing in light in the context of silence and calm had been a perception of
Coleridge's Ancient Mariner as he awoke from his terrible experiences into
a silence that sank on his heart like music. As the Mariner prayed,

> The moonlight steeped in silentness
> The steady weathercock.

The association is not unhelpful, though there is a characteristic contrast
as well as a similarity between the poetry of Wordsworth and Coleridge.
For Coleridge, the moving moon and the 'star or two beside', the
moonlight of a quiet imagination in his troubled poem, seems to temper
the Mariner's torment, some of this stemming from the bloody sun at
noon 'All in a hot and copper sky' with its 'broad and burning Face'. For
Wordsworth sunlight in his sonnet only enforces the view that we can
receive from the real, the everyday, the normal light of the sun at dawn, a
sense of blessing and of the divine.

Lambeth and the South; between two lands, England and France; between two states of being, that of the single man and that of the shortly to be married man; between time and perceptions of eternity. Yet only one thing actually moves in the sonnet. Even the hypothetical passer-by is halted by the magnificent sight. But the river moves, and Wordsworth gives a whole line to the Thames:

> The river glideth at his own sweet will.

The things of man in the sonnet are close neighboured and anchored by the permanent and elemental – earth, air, sky, fields, hills, rocks; the sun itself is energy and fire. Now water finally enters the poem. For Wordsworth, along with beauty and calmness there must be liberty in any paradisal state, and Liberty is here in the unconstrained independence and natural flow of the river. Liberty is inseparable from natural forces and the amalgam is powerful. It can be felt in another sonnet of this same August in Calais in 1802: to the negro leader and son of a slave, Toussaint L'Ouverture betrayed and imprisoned by Napoleon, Wordsworth tries to offer consolation:

> Thou hast left behind
> Powers that will work for thee; air, earth, and skies;
> There's not a breathing of the common wind
> That will forget thee ...

The Thames flowing freely is one of the powers that protect London. It is more: the river, along with the sun, is elemental and masculine, and Wordsworth, himself soon to be married, writes a line that perhaps carries a hint of Spenser's refrain in his ''Spousal Verse', *Prothalamion*, 'Sweet Thames, run softly ...'. The fair city, meanwhile, wearing only the beauty of the morning and on which the sun shines and through which the river runs, lies

> Open unto the fields, and to the sky ...

It is as though, beneath the sleeping London, there is a creative potency for life and generation, the possibility, albeit far-off, of a marriage between man's world and, in Wordsworth's phrase, 'this goodly universe'.

Not ten years before, though Wordsworth probably did not yet know it, William Blake had presented a very different Thames. Blake was not seeing the City and the river from such an unattached position as was Wordsworth; he had not the distance that a bridge affords. A Londoner among Londoners, Blake heard the Chimney-sweepers' cry and walked by the 'black'ning Churches':

> I wander thro' each charter'd street,
> Near where the charter'd Thames does flow
> And mark in every face I meet
> Marks of weakness, marks of woe.
>
> ('London', from *Songs of Experience*, 1794)

For Blake the 'mind-forged manacles' shackle man and river alike. For Wordsworth the river 'glideth at his own sweet will', just as the Derwent had flowed in his infancy, when it

> composed my thoughts
> To more than infant softness, giving me,
> Among the fretful dwellings of mankind,
> A knowledge, a dim earnest, of the calm
> Which Nature breathes among the hills and groves.
>
> (*Prelude*, 1805, I, 281-5)

Rivers run through Wordsworth's poetry, and bring calm.★

Is Wordsworth's exclamation, 'Dear God!', a thanksgiving for those fleeting glimpses of eternity that he has been able to make permanent in poetry, or is it a prayer for the people in the houses that seem still asleep? Will the 'mighty heart' that is the people in those houses awake to Blake's world of pain and mortality, to life within the dark constrictions of time? We know, and the poet knows, that the City will waken, that we do live in time, but he makes no statement. Are we troubled that Wordsworth offers us for our admiration, a city with only one person awake in it, the perceiving poet? Politics, business, the arts, orthodox religion, poverty and misery, Dorothy herself who shared the experience with him, all have receded. This is no affront to Dorothy; it was Wordsworth's belief, a belief demonstrated throughout his poetry, that we live most richly in our imaginations when we brood on our experience alone. He often in his verse turns a shared experience into a solitary one; 'I wandered lonely as a cloud' is an example. He explains in *The Prelude*,

Points have we all of us within our souls,

★Wordsworth had once before appealed to the Thames: it had been his hope in an early poem that it might bring comfort to the troubled poet William Collins; he begged the Thames

> O glide, fair stream! for ever so,
> Thy quiet soul on all bestowing,
> Till all our minds for ever flow
> As thy deep waters now are flowing.
>
> Vain thought! …
> ('Remembrance of Collins', *Lyrical Ballads*, 1800)

It would not do. Collins, imprisoned in madness, could not reach to the 'quiet soul', could not cross that bridge from the world of time to the timeless world of calm, whether of City or country, the calm which is experienced by Wordsworth in 'Composed upon Westminster Bridge'.

[32]

Where all stand single ...

(Prelude, 1805, III, 186-7)

In the sonnet the single perceiver addresses the single reader,
though thousands of individuals might read the poem.
The London held up for our contemplation has a silence
and stillness that curiously anticipates Mary Shelley's vision of
Rome, the last city lived in by the last man alive in her 1826
novel, *The Last Man*:

I entered Eternal Rome by the Porta del Popolo ... .
The wide square, the churches near, the long extent of
the Corso, the near eminence of the Trinita de' Monti
appeared like fairy work, they were so silent, so peaceful,
and so very fair. It was evening; and the population of
animals which still existed in this mighty city, had gone
to rest; there was no sound, save the murmur of its many
fountains, whose soft monotony was harmony to my
soul. The knowledge that I was in Rome soothed me;
that wondrous city, hardly more illustrious for its heroes
and sages, than for the power it exercised over the
imaginations of men. I went to rest that night; the eternal
burning of my heart quenched, – my senses tranquil.

(*The Last Man*, ed. Jane Blumberg, *The Novels of Mary Shelley*,
Pickering 1996, vol. IV, p.356)

Both writers depict the city at a transitional moment of
time: in Mary Shelley's case, evening, when night and darkness
will soon obliterate the fair and silent beauty of the 'mighty
city', just as for the last man inexorably death will claim him;
for Wordsworth the transitional time is morning; the 'mighty
heart' of the city is asleep, not dead. The potential of a whole
day is before it. It might be Blake's darkened day, but it might
not. Morning is a time of hope and it might be that the

entranced and enchanted City that Wordsworth sees briefly under the aspect of the ideal and permanent, might awaken refreshed and restored by its sleep among the free elements of nature. All the sleepers that make up the 'mighty heart' of the City – and it is the heart, the centre of feeling, that Wordsworth stresses – might wake from sleep to 'rich reward'. Significantly, in these same months of 1802, Wordsworth addresses no less than three sonnets to Sleep. Sleep

> into souls dost creep,
> Like to a breeze from heaven.
>
> ('To Sleep', 'Fond words have oft been spoken to thee')

Mary Shelley's later vision of a silent and beautiful city is a fantasy of death; Wordsworth's, though drawing seemingly towards the very deepest repose and even perhaps reminding us of the rocks and stones and trees of the final slumber of 'A slumber did my spirit seal', is far from that sleep of death. His poem is on the side of life, conscious of the good feeling that is potential within the 'mighty heart' of London, the central pulse of energy in the nation. Though no individuals move in his early morning London, they are all there, for London itself becomes a person: London wears beauty like a garment, lies like a person open to influences of fields and sky, sleeps, has power and has a heart and feelings. And it is not a fantasy. Wordsworth saw with his bodily eyes a real city, briefly under its ideal and eternal aspect as a permanent emblem of civilisation, rather as Yeats so much later was to find more exotically a symbol of permanence in the idea of Byzantium; but Wordsworth, unlike Yeats, simultaneously saw his city, London, as a real place on a specific day, a place that would soon lose its brightness in the smoke of industry and early nineteenth-century living, but could, like any person, contain

                    ... a heart
        That watches and receives.
              ('The Tables Turned')

Wordsworth's poem of course makes no statements, offers no
meanings. We have no painterly description, only fragments of
pictures, images. It is these that sustain the soul while, all
around our reading, meanings suggest themselves, hover, and
give place to other meanings, acceptable, inconsistent,
contradictory; it hardly matters. The words offer images in
space and light, and these remain. The words, paradoxically,
also convey silence, and this remains. Wordsworth lets us sense
through words the powerful good of silence, stillness and
calm; it is a poet's gift. Within this poetic crossing of Westminster Bridge, Wordsworth has used expression to convey the
necessity of silence, to reveal within the movement that is
inseparable from transition, from crossing a bridge, the
intensity, not of doing or moving, but of being, of being still.

III

London was to continue to inspire Wordsworth. Within four
days of the title date, 3 September, of 'Westminster Bridge', the
Wordsworths dined on 7 September 1802 with Charles and
Mary Lamb; 'I was their guide', wrote Charles Lamb on 8
September, 'to Bartlemy Fair!' It was two years before
Wordsworth wrote his impressions of Bartholomew Fair, the
annual fourteen-day festival held at Smithfield:

              ... what a hell
        For eyes and ears! what anarchy and din
        Barbarian and infernal ...

Charles Lamb by Robert Hancock, 1798

He was driven to writing blank verse lines like lists,

> ... chattering monkeys dangling from their poles,
> And children whirling in their roundabouts;
>   ... buffoons against buffoons
> Grimacing, writhing, screaming ...
> Equestrians, Tumblers, Women, Girls, and Boys,
> Blue-breeched, pink-vested, and with towering plumes.
> – All moveables of wonder from all parts,
> Are here, Albinos, painted Indians, Dwarfs,
> The Horse of Knowledge, and the learned Pig,
> The Stone-eater, the Man that swallows fire,
> Giants, Ventriloquists, the Invisible Girl,
> The Bust that speaks, and moves its goggling eyes,
> The Wax-work, Clock-work ...

(*Prelude*, 1805, VII, 668-86)

Thomas Rowlandson and Augustus Charles Pugin, Bartholomew Fair, 1808

And so on; an evocation that fascinates by its energy even as Wordsworth characterises it as 'This Parliament of Monsters'. It is at quite the opposite end of his London experience from that of the sonnet.

A more temperate view, and probably one about everyday London that Wordsworth was fairly able to sustain was the view that had been his from his very first entry into 'the great City'. He was probably at the time eighteen years old, and he recalled the moment in 1804:

> On the Roof
> Of an itinerant Vehicle I sate,
> With vulgar men about me, vulgar forms
> Of houses, pavements, streets, of men and things,
> Mean shapes on every side …
> A weight of Ages did at once descend

Upon my heart ...
        ... weight and power,
          ... I only now
Remember that it was a thing divine.

                (Prelude, 1805, VIII, 693-710)

Wordsworth, thus early, a Cambridge undergraduate, probably in 1788, was seeing the world from the top of a Coach, and he saw and felt no such grandeur entering London as he was later to feel from the coach roof on Westminster Bridge. There was nothing splendid, but nevertheless he looked past the immediate appearance of 'Mean shapes on every side', of commonplace houses and people, and became aware, beyond first impressions, not, admittedly, of the City's 'mighty heart', but of the force of history, the 'weight of Ages'. Only when writing his autobiographical poem some fifteen years later in 1804 does he remember that this sense of 'weight and power', momentary as it was, 'was a thing divine'.

The idea of London was potent; it gave Wordsworth a sense

> Of what had been here done, and suffered here
> Through ages, and was doing, suffering, still ...
>
>   *(ibid.*, 782-3)

The place, he says,

> Was thronged with impregnations, like those wilds
> In which my early feelings had been nursed,
> And naked valleys, full of caverns, rocks
> And audible seclusions, dashing lakes,
> Echoes and Waterfalls, and pointed crags
> That into music touch the passing wind.
>
>   *(ibid.*, 791-96)

One sees again that equation of City and country that has such force in the sonnet. In the *Prelude* Wordsworth reveals how it was by taking thought that he reached this position, by having knowledge, and by considering the effect of the past upon the present. What is thought out in the *Prelude* was compelling and sudden vision in the sonnet.

'Earth has not any thing to shew more fair' is unique within Wordsworth's writing for its power to penetrate directly into what T.S. Eliot, tossed upon the hypocrisies and confusions of modern London, would call 'the heart of light, the silence'. Eliot could manage this glimpse of blessedness in his *Waste Land* only for a brief moment and only by an act of memory; but for Wordsworth in his sonnet it was an unquestioned reality.

Something of the same experience was to be Wordsworth's six years later. He was then not on a coach either entering the City or crossing the Thames, he was not with Dorothy. He was walking alone towards the City of London one Sunday in April 1808 about 7 in the morning. He had parted in some trouble of mind from Coleridge and was

… noticing nothing, and entirely occupied with my own thoughts, when looking up, I saw before me the avenue of Fleet street, silent, empty, and pure white, with a sprinkling of new-fallen snow, not a cart or Carriage to obstruct the view, no noise, only a few soundless and dusky foot-passengers, here and there; you remember the elegant curve of Ludgate Hill in which this avenue would terminate, and beyond and towering above it was the huge and majestic form of St Pauls, solemnised by a thin veil of falling snow. I cannot say how much I was affected at this unthought-of sight, in such a place and what a blessing I felt there is in habits of exalted Imagination. My sorrow was controlled, and my uneasiness of

The everyday view of St Paul's by Thomas Girtin, 1775–1802, the 'familiar spot' which the falling snow transformed for Wordsworth into a 'visionary scene'. Watercolour reproduced by kind permission of Thomas Agnew & Sons Ltd.

mind not quieted and relieved altogether, seemed at once to receive the gift of an anchor of security.

(from a letter to Sir George Beaumont, 8 April 1808)

This is a fine account, particularly in the specific narrative part ending with the 'veil of falling snow', and it tells a story Wordsworth has told before: that of the abstracted mind, unnoticing, suddenly confronted with something other, a visionary power almost, that takes over. Wordsworth has written it in 'A Night-Piece', in 'The Discharged Soldier', and he was shortly to make a poem out of this London experience. He wrote this letter from Grasmere only two days after arriving home, and he tells Sir George that since his return he has 'scarcely greeted or noticed the beautiful vale in which we live ... some of the imagery of London has ... been more present to my mind'. So present was it that before summer was over he had told the story of his encounter with St Paul's:

> Pressed with conflicting thoughts of love and fear
> I parted from thee, Friend! and took my way
> Through the great City, pacing with an eye
> Downcast, ear sleeping, and feet masterless
> That were sufficient guide unto themselves,
> And step by step went pensively. Now, mark!
> Not how my trouble was entirely hushed,
> (That might not be) but how by sudden gift,
> Gift of Imagination's holy power,
> My soul in her uneasiness received
> An anchor of stability. It chanced
> That while I thus was pacing I raised up
> My heavy eyes and instantly beheld,
> Saw at a glance in that familiar spot,
> A visionary scene – a length of street
> Laid open in its morning quietness,

Deep, hollow, unobstructed, vacant, smooth,
And white with winter's purest white, as fair,
As fresh and spotless as he ever sheds
On field or mountain. Moving Form was none
Save here and there a shadowy Passenger,
Slow, shadowy, silent, dusky, and beyond
And high above this winding length of street,
This noiseless and unpeopled avenue,
Pure, silent, solemn, beautiful, was seen
The huge majestic Temple of St Paul
In awful sequestration, through a veil,
Through its own sacred veil of falling snow.

By contrast with this leisurely blank verse, the compression of 'Composed upon Westminster Bridge, 3 Sept. 1802' is the more exhilarated and radiant. Yet there are connections. The silence, the sudden unexpected gift of vision, the street 'laid open in its morning quietness', the purity, the stillness, the comparison with the freshness of field or mountain, the noiseless and unpeopled streets, these seem features of the earlier sonnet; at the same time the uneasiness of the viewer, the shadowiness, the accumulating negatives, the whiteness with no sunshine, the 'shadowy Passenger, Slow, shadowy', have all a ghostly presence as though London has become an underworld. Through a veil, even though a sacred veil, of falling snow, we see looming, even oppressive,

The huge majestic Temple of St Paul
In awful sequestration ...

In different ways both 'St Paul's' and the sonnet fulfil a central definition by Coleridge of one of Wordsworth's strengths: to give 'the charm of novelty to things of every day', to awaken 'the mind's attention from the lethargy of custom', and direct

S. T. Coleridge by Thomas Phillips, 1818

it 'to the loveliness and the wonders of the world before us', to remove 'the film of familiarity' (*Biographia Literaria*, 1817, chapter 14). Two familiar London vistas, that from Westminster Bridge, and that of the dome of St Paul's above Ludgate Hill, are freshened for us, made new to our imaginations.

But Wordsworth never published 'St Paul's'. And we might agree with his decision. With some of the same features this later poem is not a rewritten 'Westminster Bridge'. The force and the ecstasy have gone. In 'St Paul's' Wordsworth no longer leaves the reader only with images and feelings; he explains, he tells us in so many words how the sudden vision works upon the mind, and what its consequence was upon the poet's mood. We are told, perhaps, too much, and we are told too soon; before we have had the story we are given the lesson.

It was perfect for Dorothy in her prose Journal to mention the one dome by name, St Paul's, and it was right for

Wordsworth in his sonnet not to speak the name, but to refer in the plural to 'Ships, towers, domes, theatres and temples', to make his City grand and universal. His later focus in 'St Paul's' upon a close view seems less happy. While the lines 'St Paul's' are scarcely known, the sonnet 'Composed upon Westminster Bridge, Sept 3 1803 [1802]' found admirers straight away when it came out in *Poems in Two Volumes*, 1807. Wordsworth placed it carefully: preceding the 'Westminster Bridge' sonnet he printed another sonnet written also about the calm that is in nature and is healing to the troubled poet. This is entitled 'Written in very early youth', and it balances the 'Westminster Bridge' morning sonnet, because it is written about that other time of transition, evening. It was composed even perhaps when Wordsworth was still a schoolboy. Much revised he published it entitled 'Written at Evening' in the newspaper *The Morning Post* on 13 February 1802, only some three months before his new awakening to the sonnet form when Dorothy read him some of Milton's sonnets in May. The first line in both the early and the 1807 versions of the sonnet is the same:

Calm is all nature as a resting wheel.

In the poem a slumber steals over nature and the poet seems comforted. He begs his friends to leave him to himself for his grief is best allayed when alone and within the darkening 'blank of things' of nature at rest.

After this moody melancholy sonnet, 'Earth has not any thing to shew more fair' on the next page opens like an explosion. This poem offers no fashionable literary calmness but a calmness with all the tension of a great City round it, a calmness and beauty daringly elevated above that of the first morning in the finest new created garden of the world, a calmness so deep and yet so tenuous that like persons asleep who will soon waken into life, the calm is just held, and because of that it is astonishingly precious. It will not last; only in eternity could so vast an innocence be sustained. With this mortal awareness the viewer carries the reader from that first bursting astonishment at the City's beauty through to a deep sense of calm, and of wonder that these things can be. They will not last, yet of course they do. They are in the words of the poem.

II.   37 Sonnets

Introduction

Peter and Alice Oswald

WE WERE DELIGHTED when the Globe asked us, almost a year ago, to commission a series of sonnets on Westminster Bridge. We saw this as a way to link the theatre to its context, using the sonnet as the quickest route from Shakespeare's Globe to Wordsworth's bridge, and from there to wherever we are now. For this reason we asked poets to respond not so much to Wordsworth's poem as to the bridge and its view, using any variation of the sonnet form. Since the idea was to push that form to its limits, we sought out poets of contrasting styles: from those who use regular metre to those who don't even use regular words; prose poets, verse playwrights, unpublished poets and a folk singer. We hope you find the resulting collection as varied as thirty-seven sonnets on one theme can possibly be.

JOHN AGARD

Toussaint L'Ouverture Acknowledges
Wordsworth's Sonnet 'To Toussaint L'Ouverture'

I have never walked on Westminster Bridge
or had a close-up view of daffodils.
My childhood's roots are the Haitian hills
where runaway slaves made a freedom pledge
and scarlet poincianas flaunt their scent.
I have never walked on Westminster Bridge
or speak, like you, with Cumbrian accent.
My tongue bridges Europe to Dahomey.
Yet how sweet is the smell of liberty
when human beings share a common garment.
So thanks, brother, for your sonnet's tribute.
May it resound when the Thames' text stays mute.
And what better ground than a city's bridge
for my unchained ghost to trumpet love's decree.

PATIENCE AGBABI

The London Eye

Through my gold-tinted Gucci sunglasses,
the sightseers. Big Ben's quarter chime
strikes the convoy of number 12 buses
that bleeds into the city's monochrome.

Through somebody's zoom lens, me shouting
to you, 'Hello! ... on ... bridge ... 'minster!'
The aerial view postcard, the man writing
squat words like black cabs in rush hour.

The South Bank buzzes with a rising treble.
You kiss my cheek, formal as a blind date.
We enter Cupid's Capsule, a thought bubble
where I think, 'Space age!', you think, 'She was late.'

Big Ben strikes six, my SKIN .Beat blinks, replies
18·02. We're moving anti-clockwise.

CAROLINE BERGVALL

Bridged foot, 30 September 2002

: Pushed along the structure hanging
left right left
: right across sharp susp
ended lights increase the river
: , , ambient traffic art trades
limbs, borders, co-option, language, lies and
, ; I have debts
. things left
behind thoughts I dont
, , ; write lines dont cross not
' , , ! riskd fall low fell short
: on crossing a my-foot lifts metal dust
 ! ; All that shines in the dark
! doesnt march in step

SEAN BORODALE

From Westminster

I walked from night into day, and I passed
a man alone, I saw he bit his tongue.
I walked into clear light. Shade flew up fast,
I saw the river there, curled waters ran.
Unholy tigers flashed up through the Thames,
a shepherd's love was all the bridge across.
And wolves of towers, flows of blackened streams,
and lambs of pity loved were London's cursed.
I passed a woman singing to herself
a song, it ran before her like a lamb.
Her lamb of song was dark with bleating grief.
Below, the driven Thames flowed red as blood;
the sun, I saw the burning sun drive love
into the hearts of lambs, and passed in dread.

ANDY BROWN

Westminster Bridge as 'The Bridge of Lies'

The Bridge of Lies, in Sibiu, Romania, where lovers go
to make their marriage proposals, because no lie may be
told upon the bridge.

We meet each other half way, catch the sky
blush pink, like lovers on the *Bridge of Lies*
who come to hear inviolate proposals.
I start to ask, but look into the sun
& drop the thread of what I mean to say.
Its shadow sinks beneath the Thames's pull;
emerges elsewhere on the esplanade,
as out of breath as me. The asking's done.
As when Romantic Masters flattened out
the middle-ground before their landscapes rose
to castles set on crenellated heights,
the moment slips away toward St. Pauls.
You lift yourself, to whisper, onto toes,
sing 'Yes' into my left ear's ringing bowl.

MATTHEW CALEY

No Bulwark

*'Alas, English poesie may now be defined
as Andrew Motion recalled in tranquillity'*
HARRY NOVACK

Listen up, behold the tableau: two crackheads and their spoonlit
    underchins
        'neath the doubled alcove of a riverbridge
not elegised by sonneteers, not pendant with Papal-clerks.
    Peripheral figures – in any other play they would be
gravediggers, they
            are gravediggers –

saying one to the other: *fuck it, feel the hit, fuck it, feel the hit*
    repeatedly
        in slurred pentameters, their vision clouds, occludes, chiaroscuro.
Neo-Turner with fireworks, a scorch-orange sunset boils the
    water's runny neon,
            boils their brows,
inside the littered den – dogbones, acetylene-torch, unlit, *Empire*
    magazine-
            cover star Luke Skywalker, shoulder torn,

no epaulettes. *Yet there's a bridge they hold up in their minds that span
    -s no stream or river, parts for no vast ships with fragrant prows,
has no flying buttresses at either end but vast supports of air*

it sways, buckles – *fuck it, feel the hit* – a match, a flare, a blow,
    a nostril salts with sea-froth like a Marguerita, an iris issues arcs
of welding-sparks, a bridge with no support, a greyscale rainbow.

CIARAN CARSON

Claude Monet, The Thames
Below Westminster, 1871

*the Franco-Prussian War broke out in the
summer of 1870; in the autumn, Monet
fled to London with his wife, Camille
Doncieux, and their three-year-old son*

in the Houses

of Parliament fog

two tug-

boats drowse

upon the wooden pier

three stick

figures black

silhouettes appear

light shaped

and broken

by the river

Monet has escaped

the unspoken

War

KATE CLANCHY

On Westminster Bridge

I often used to come up here. I like
this diffuse light, the quiet passage
of the river. You get a sense of order:
the sun discreet, high-up, a copper
gleam in pewter, touching the roof-tops,
the brick checks in Lambeth Palace,
with the chalk strokes of a master.
Church and State are still and opposite.
An aqua tint. A pop-up map for tourists.
Which is me, today. Up from the provinces
with a push chair and a baby on a day-trip.
I hold him up to the parapet
for some time in silence. 'Big,' he says.
'Is big. Big, big, big, big. Is big. It is.'

ROBERT CRAWFORD

Westminster Bridge

Strangers come each day to walk on water,
Confirmed as who they are by showers and light.
Some time I'd like to stroll here with my daughter,
Cheerfully Anglophile. I'd see each sight
Through Monet's eyes, staring across Thames mudshine
At European London in the rain,
A parliamonarchy that isn't mine
But still feels close. Now, though, I want my train.
Tonight I'll go to bed in Euston Station
Dreaming myself over the sleepers, north
Into my rainy European nation
But when at 4 a.m. I cross the Forth
Bridge, I'll raise the blind and love each raindrop
That's passportless and free and falls non-stop.

MICHAEL DONAGHY

Midriver

– and is a bridge: Now to [both ways] Then:
child to lolly: spark across the wire:
lover to the target of desire:
Lambeth to Westminster: back again.
Verb's a vector not a monument,
but someone skipped a stone across this river
fixing its trajectory forever
in seven arches after the event
– so stops halfway and, neither there nor there,
but cold and rained on and intransitive,
watches London switch from *when* to *where*,
why to silence in the traffic jam,
thinks *I can see the borough where I live
but here is temporarily who I am.*

IAN DUHIG

Vilbia

I

"*Qui mihi Vilbiam involavit sic*
Liquat como do aqua.★ Lay it on thick;
He thought of nothing but his own sweet will,
So with a vengeance now I wish him ill!"

II

He got to where he'd say he's come to love me
When suddenly, mid-lie, he stalled above me.
Thinning like air great heat was making shiver,
He held for a second, a bridge of glass,
Realized the horror coming to pass
Then pissed himself from ice to raging river,
Breaking on me in his undoing birth
That pulled him back inside his mother earth.

III

I put on a clean robe. I spoke a prayer.
Then I washed that man right out of my hair.

★ A curse from the Romano-Celtic period discovered in
Bath. Cut backwards onto a strip of lead, it means, "May he
who carried off Vilbia from me become as liquid as water".

AIDAN ANDREW DUN

Bridging

Down by the river stands a giant tree,
a century towering there in silence.
A girder of the natural world must be
the greying prisoner of its eminence.
But look where a wooden viaduct of green
transcends the basic root-life underneath,
ornament of the void, this serene
lonely reaching-out of the furthest leaf.
Here is our transmarine! All people, regard
the bridge from one side to the other run.
To span a different zone of air is hard.
We all shall overpass before we are done.
She comes to meet us on a bridge, they say,
upon the crossing of that final day.

PAUL FARLEY

A Great Stink

. . . but in fifty years the Commons will complain
they can't sit in this river's smell, and soak
their curtains in chloride of lime to take
the edge off what they'll liken to a drain.
'King Cholera' will rise from *Punch* and walk
abroad with a peg on his nose. No poetry
will get written, save those olfactory
pieces papers commission: *This smell's a baulk*
to anything the eye can register
and crossing here is hazardous to health
at dawn, when all the night soil of Westminster
meets with a flood tide. Citizens of wealth,
flee for the summer while the city festers
and strike out for the coast like merde *yourselves.*

PETER FINCH

N Wst Brdg
30902

erth nt a thng so brill
hes dul v soul pssng by
sght of mjstic tch
cty now wrs grmnts
of mrng bty :-) slnt bare
Shps twrs dms thtrs + chrchs
opn t flds + sky - ^v^v^
brite glttrng in nosmke air
nvr sun so butfl steep
n hs 1st splndr vlly rck or hll
nvr saw nvr flt clm so deep!!!
rvr flws at hs sweet wll (own):
Deer GD! vry hses seem slp | |
+ all tht BIG HRT lyng still!

JANE GRIFFITHS

The Bridge

is a broadside, a centuries' matter of course
or palimpsest, so many have set their sights
on it, and the disposable cameras show gaslights,
and arches skimmed like stones under horse-
drawn carriages. Someone's for Parliament Square.
Someone's for Battersea. It's easy; it's the shortest
distance between two points over a crow's nest
of workmen, and their building neither here nor there
and the bridge a force of habit it's hard to climb
down from under the wheeling eye and all that motion
(trampolinists somersault over County Hall) or turn
from to the level of the first man on the shoreline
whose river was a height, and whose stones, enormous
boulders where he balanced, casting for a way across.

SOPHIE HANNAH

On Westminster Bridge

I don't believe the building of a bridge
Should be an image that belongs to peace.
Raised eyebrow or the river's hardened ridge,
It wouldn't want hostilities to cease.
Aloof, on tiptoes, it deserts each side
For the high ground and, though it has to touch
Land that real lives have made undignified,
I don't believe it likes that very much.
It knows that every time we try to cross
To a new place, old grudges bind our feet.
It holds out little hope and feels no loss,
Indifferent more than neutral, when we meet
Halfway to transfer ownership of blame,
Then both of us go back the way we came.

JANE HILL

Liminal

It lies south of here; a concluded shape
held together with language and old pictures.
Your aerated state – found only on bridges –
untwists this moment. Your mind makes
fourteen piers of Portland stone, their stays
rotting away like teeth from the root upward.
Girls are Winchester geese, propped leery for
a slow fight under the hoods of the balustrade
in case of rain. They show one thigh; white as feathers
in the light. Ambitious men, building a circus on
a diamond, pick tricks from the sandy dirt among
the marks of boots. Old watchman, severed
from his post, leaks stab wounds in a drunken brawl;
two brothers running from his pitched-out sprawl

left on the central span, reach the far shore.
He dies. A scholar sparks electric charge,
a circuit stretched between his Leyden jars
and the new clock hangs and quarters every hour.
You evolve and evolve. There is the same
low-tide river smell as the breeze skims the mud
and the boom of modern traffic is like blood
pumping through your head. And now the range
caught by the eye defines your boundary,
the sound of footsteps breaking up towards the sea.

ASHLEY HUTCHINGS

What god am I?

What god am I that I can gamely fit
A thousand scurrying souls upon my back
And bear them from a place they wish to quit
To one they more desire, without a crack
Appearing on my worn and weathered face?

The years and generations too I span;
I've learned to take the ever-quickening pace
That beats a rhythm like no drummer can
Within my wise and other-worldly stride.

Thus movement is the substance of my song;
The tide beneath and high above, the throng;
And here a Parliament is changing face,
And there a Globe's revolving in its pride,
While I observe and serve with God-like grace.

BRENDAN KENNELLY

Dorothy Wordsworth and Westminster Bridge

Beside the fire he sits with half-closed eyes
(In a drench of sleep I saw a happy place)
He spoke this morning of the Bridge's beauty
(I thought of a woman with a jolly red face)
Such a view, he said, no man has ever seen
(Yesterday an old man called, gaunt and grey)
How could such a city be made by men?
(I gave the old man bacon. He went his way).

A scene like this, he said, can never die
(I made bread, batter pudding, rhubarb tart)
It will outlive the purest poem or story
(Bullfinches wingdance in a twittering sky)
He wonders how a Bridge can steal a heart
(He'll marry soon. She listens well, dark Mary).

JOANNA LAURENS

Bridge of Sound

By the sunflowers in the steep of night
a breath, a breath again, an unsaid name
brought the full moon up negative white
on yellow heads, on fifty fields the same;
and in the wet cave near the crash of sea
a digger stilled his pick and stood to hear
the breathed unsaid (the name which was to be
dropped and lost, spoken stopped) now echo free,
voiced by rock to bandy about the man,
who doubted it, shook his head, took his pick
and killed the noise; with a hit overran
the word, dug a grave, sent it to ground quick.
The dull thud of his tool; the hocks of ground;
the sunflowers; the moon sunk and no sound.

KONA MACPHEE

Flying to London

In the air two hours, at my left hand
I watched the sunset's awning-blinds unroll
across the Great Red Centre's rusty folds,
tracing a bas-relief of sky and ground.
Between those lines that marked us outward-bound,
I read a truth my country won't be told:
what foreignness our textbook England holds
couldn't be less like home than this harsh land.
In fogless dawn, real London scrolls below
and wrests itself from History and Lit
with houses ranked grey row, grey row, grey row
and proto-traffic stacking on the streets.
The seatbelt light comes on; the plane banks low;
its engines spill a last Australian heat.

JAMIE MCKENDRICK

A Shattered Bridge

Trouble with bridges is cows like to come
and shit on them was Jan Masaryk's riposte
to Beneš's hope the Czechlands might become
a kind of bridge between East and West.
That was before his trouble with windows
– launched of his own accord, according
to Gottwald, from one high up the bleak
façade of Černínský palác, its thirty pillars recording
the Thirty Years War, onto the rose, grey and black
cobblestones tourists now like to take home.
Relics bedded like molars in cold soil,
their rough cubes more picturesque than Berlin Wall.
The Ministry of Foreign Affairs' carpark
now stands on the stones on which he fell –

– facing the Loreto where a single brick
dislodged from Mary's house in Nazareth
was flown by angel couriers this far north.
The vaulted niches of the courtyard wear
a collectable series of Marian apparitions:
borne by cherubs she descends like a seed-case
into chilly windswept landscapes with their place-names
on scrolls in Czech and German. The wounded skies
above a dwarfed village and a field of cows,
a disappointed bridge or shattered pier,
seem to weep pine resin or gum arabic.
Upstairs, in glass cases, lie the cobbled pearl
crucifixes, the diamond monstrance, the coral pyxes
held together by filigree braces and bridgework.

EDWIN MORGAN

Sometime upon Westminster Bridge

The swollen Thames raced east and smelt the sea.
The sea was howling, and in driven rain
Spread westward like an unrelenting stain.
The shattered Barrier swung loose and free.
Sludge weltered where the tourist piers should be.
Hungerford collapsed with a full train
Crying and shrieking in mad fear and pain,
Bundled below to wet eternity.
Never did moon more balefully look down
On crumbling barn and mashed-out cattle-ford.
Westminster Bridge is sinking, left to drown
In mud and night with all its souls on board.
The great clock hears its last chime shiver down
Among the chilly dead, the silent horde.

ROBERT NYE

Dorothy Wordsworth's Sonnet

William was on his way to say good-bye
To his French mistress and their natural child.
The weather, I remember, was quite mild,
Though a bright sun shone fiercely in the sky.
My brother sat, as usual, silently,
Wrapt in his cloak a-top the Dover coach,
Annette upon his mind. I dared not broach
That subject, so I spoke of purity—
Directing his attention to the way
The morning light redeemed the dirty city
Seen from Westminster Bridge. (I could not say
How much I loved him, which was no great pity.)
'Tomorrow will improve on yesterday,'
I told him. 'Look, the prospect's almost pretty!'

SEAN O'BRIEN

Sonnet on Westminster Bridge

We all love a bridge, its ideal nowhere
Dreamed by physics from the secret bed.
Imagine this one speaking truth to power –
Who did what to whom, who should be dead,
The whole exchange, the names, the jam, the jism
Spilled by losers idling on the edge
Before the journalists and frogmen come
To shake their heads at erring privilege.

But this is just a bridge. It takes no views.
Impassive and civilian, its task
Is to be crossed and trodden on for good,
The royal road from the salons to the stews,
Where ministers can breathe without a mask,
And say they smell no shit. But then they would.

March 2002

ALICE OSWALD

Westminster Bridge

go and glimpse the lovely inattentive water
discarding the gaze of many a bored street walker

where the weather trespasses into strip-lit offices
through tiny windows into tiny thoughts and authorities

and the soft beseeching tapping of typewriters

take hold of a breath-width instant, stare
at water which is already elsewhere
in a scrapwork of flashes and glittery flutters
and regular waves of apparently motionless motion

under the teetering structures of administration

where a million shut-away eyes glance once
restlessly at the river's ruts and glints

count five, then wander swiftly
away over the stone wing-bone of the city

PETER OSWALD

Sonnet On Westminster Bridge

Trickles of thinking mingle with the flow
From pipes of every kind. On my left hand
Westminster bickers as the waters go
Carrying off the loose parts of the land;
This town will stain my ghost when I am gone
If I do not scour off into the brown
Flowers beneath my feet, all I have done,
Shake it off doglike, let it all go down
Into the squeezed-out city's boil of poisons
Stirred to one colour by the rush to ocean,
Seepage released from cinemas and prisons,
Rainwater rainbowed from the roads' commotion;
Drain my whole mind that the returning tide
Will bring me back, I hope, sea-bright, sea-wide.

RUTH PADEL

Like Rosin Across Flame

Her back to Southwark Bridge, she's watching lollipops of
   light
Butter up the khaki river. Tourists in colours of jacaranda,
Peepul, golmohur are queueing for the Globe: in whose
   original
(Lost along New Globe Walk, where power-drills are
   foaming
Mirages of Real Stone dust) stage-hands blew rosin across
   flame
To make false lightning. She's going to meet him here, Bovis
Site entrance on the cement pier. What'll it be like, to stroll
Through sunlight with the guy whose heart she made her
   home in

All those years: whom she kept alive? When the mobile goes,
   it brings
The whole lot back. His *mise en scène*: fake linnet-calls of
   Arden
From behind the painted roof. Standing her up, letting her
   down.
Comedy or tragedy, you put your sad song in Act IV, or
   maybe V.
The one about trust, or truth; and what a clown
You were, to sally forth on *that* white hobby horse again.

JACOB POLLEY

The Distance

I feel your heart through the back of the chair –
yes, it's me, standing over your shoulder
as you pass your hand over your hair
like a card-sharp or conjuror,
breaking the joints of a stiff new deck.
There are cities, ports, into whose harbours
drift whole districts with their ballrooms and kitchens;
places where the earth is cracked open
and men climb down with their own minds
thrown out in front of them:
so what should you care
if I dipped one hand into the current
and changed the course of your black hair,
the better to hold my breath to your throat?

PETER REDGROVE

Long Sonnet

Love is ripe beyond bearing
        it must go to seed
                the Speaker pulls at his bottle:
It is one of his bridges
        joining eros with nous;
                the weeping Thatcher
Is high-minded in white
        then drenches with hot black emotion
                so the Seer pulls at his bottle:
He is on both sides of the river
        at once, he chooses
                the pivotal centre, Housewatching,
Leans over the backwards-flowing water
        and the frontal flow,
                where he pulls at his bottle;
May Maggie the Moon-Goddess of Moods
        be restored to her majority
                says the Seer-speaker who pulls
At his bottle
        for it is a shock to understand
                all the Ministers have
Taken to drink, like always:
        the river is a mighty majority flowing
                past the Tower of Right-Timing,
Her brother erect, who chimes;
        now the division-bell rings
                like transfiguration.

DENISE RILEY

Composed Underneath Westminster Bridge
April 4th 2002

Broad gravel barges shove the drift; each wake
Thwacks these stone steps. A rearing tugboat streaked
Past moorhens dabbing floss, spun pinkish-beaked.
Peanuts in caramelised burnt chocolate bake
Through syrupy air; above, fried onions cake.
Pigeons on steeleyed dates neck-wrestle, piqued,
Oblivious to their squabs who whined and squeaked
In iron-ringed nests, nursed in high struts. Opaque
Brown particles swarm churning through the tide.
That navy hoop of cormorant can compose
A counter to this shield – eagles splayed wide,
Gold martlets – on the bridge's side: it glows
While through the eau-de-nil flaked arches slide
The boats Bert Prior and The Eleanor Rose.

PENELOPE SHUTTLE

Bridge Spiel

I'm the bridge without a sigh.
When you were a child, I was where London began,
not at Waterloo or the walk towards me and my buses.

When the big clock strikes
I don't bat an ear,
hours are too little for the time zone of me.

I minister to north and south,
linking two sets of actors,
those in Parliament, those at the Globe.

I'm the bridge where anyone can stand,
no charge, not even for a poet.

Best come here on a busy night for stargazers
or at dawn's flummox of gold
before the homeless are up and sighing.

JOHN STAMMERS

Composed on the Millennium Bridge on the
Morning of Its Reopening 22nd February 2002

City of random architectures, effluvia and bridge
in which we debouch onto the new Millennium:
Plexiglas, hawser and the old marriage
of the here and now to the wide world's conundrum.
I study the high-boned colourings of your face,
hot medallions in a cold circumstance;
my words scream out in the torque and race
of wind, *'scape this temporal 'cumbrance*,
or whatever. My god, what is is neither fair
nor foul nor favourable, I say, before the spot where
you ask, 'Why leave for a thing you already have?'
Circumspice and the blue-blue neon on the blue air
tops out the buildings, fashionably, there to here.
I say, 'Because', then 'the way over is the way back.'

GRETA STODDART

After (or before) *The Fall*

"O young woman, throw yourself into the water again so that
I may a second time have the chance of saving both of us!"
The Fall, Albert Camus

Here? No, I wouldn't. Not that I care
in reality, but there is something to be said
(and you probably said it) for doing it where –
but I'm thinking now that what you wrote I read
far too young, or is it from birth this urge
to jump and lose oneself in the inky river?
Look. I'm at it again, deep in character;
I grip the rail, my heart knocks with knowledge.

Where are you now, Jean-Baptiste Clamence,
with your book-length excuse and elaborate confession?
Too late. Save your words. Stay on the shelf

for I've dropped your plot and find myself entranced
with mine – this will she won't she loop of dying,
this well-worn fiction, like walking on water, or flying.

PAUL STUBBS

Westminster Bridge 2002

I walk out onto this bridge, awkwardly,
as if up onto my very own bone-stilts.
Peering through chinks in the upcoming crowd.

At each body alternating the gait of
me; and the reflection of the city:
an old wreck resurfacing, bobbing up

past the scum and corpses of the thames.
Where beneath me it gives slow monotonous
chase to itself. And where at my feet

now the wind it borrows a crisp-packet
for a lung; where the commuters put not one foot wrong
in the dance of day; until when suddenly,

the traffic it halts, quickening the crowd,
forcing the bodies by, in masks, in shrouds . . .

CHARLES TOMLINSON

Westminster Bridge from the Eye

What is a sonnet? "Take these fourteen lines
Of *Paradise Lost*," Wordsworth told a friend –
(A gathering music with no rhymes to end
Each line) "The image of a sphere or dewdrop,
An orbicular body," he went on.
This sonnet – globe within The Globe – is one
Way to double the sonnet circle. Take
The Eye also. From its orbicular cabins
You see Westminster Bridge extend as he
Never saw it – the same bridge with its view
Where ships, towers, domes, theatres lie below,
And now that clambering disparity –
Corbusier's children quarreling for the sky –
In a paradise lost that Wordsworth did not know.

SARAH WARDLE

On Westminster Bridge

Pause for a moment on Westminster Bridge,
freeze the Thames, turn passing cars to stone,
suspend the rain, still the speedboat's flag,
stop the Prime Minister in mid-flow,
cast the people in bronze, anchor the barge,
say *Sleep* to a vendor in a hot dog van,
shut the London Eye, let a gull not budge,
remove the battery from Big Ben.
Now hold it there for two hundred years,
the time it would take us to travel upstream
to Wordsworth, and further on to Shakespeare,
or down to the twenty-third century.
Shrink the present into fourteen lines.
Sign your sonnet and post it on the tide.

Poets' Biographies

John Agard, poet and playwright, was born in Guyana and came to the UK in 1977. He has written many books for children and adults and was the BBC Writer in Residence in 1998. His latest volume, *Weblines*, was published by Bloodaxe in 2000, and his children's collection, *The Animals Would Like a Word With You*, won a Smarties Award in 1996.

Patience Agbabi was born in London in 1965 to Nigerian parents. A much sought-after performer and workshop facilitator, her publications include the groundbreaking *R.A.W.* (Gecko Press, 1995) and *Transformatrix* (Payback Press, 2000). She is Associate Lecturer in Creative Writing at Cardiff University.

Caroline Bergvall is a poet whose texts include *ECLAT* (Sound & Language, 1996) and *Goan Atom, 1* (Krupskaya, 2001). She has developed a number of text-performances in collaboration with other artists. She is Associate Research Fellow at Dartington College of Arts, Devon.

Sean Borodale is an artist and poet who has had work published in various journals and magazines. He was Artist in Residence at the Wordsworth Trust in 1999, where he curated the exhibition *Walking to Paradise*. He has recently been Guest Artist of the Rijksakademie in the Netherlands.

Andy Brown is Lecturer in Creative Writing at Exeter University. His third collection, *From a Cliff*, is published by Arc (July 2002). He co-produced *Of Science* (Worple Press, 2001) with David Morley. The editor of *Binary Myths: Vols 1 and 2* (Stride), he also Directed Totleigh Barton for six years for the Arvon Foundation.

Matthew Caley's first full-length collection, *Thirst*, was published by Slow Dancer in 1999 and was nominated for the Forward Prize for Best First Collection. Recently his work has been commended in the National Poetry Competition and received special mention in the TLS/Blackwells Competition.

Ciaran Carson was born in Belfast in 1948 and is the author of seven collections of poetry, including *The Irish for No* (1987) and *Opera Et Cetera* (1996), both published by Bloodaxe. His prose works include *Fishing for Amber* (1999) and his most recent novel is 2001's *Shamrock Tea* (Granta). He is a past winner of both the T S Eliot Prize and the prestigious Irish Times Literature Prize.

Kate Clanchy won a Forward Prize and the Somerset Maugham Award for her first collection *Slattern* (Chatto, 1995). Currently working as a freelance writer and broadcaster, her most recent volume is *Samarkand* (Picador, 1999).

Robert Crawford is the author of many books, including several collections of verse – the most recent being 1999's *Spirit Machines* (Cape). He has co-edited with Simon Armitage the *Penguin Book of Poetry from Britain and Ireland since 1945*, and, with Mick Imlah, the *New Penguin Book of Scottish Verse* (2001). He teaches at the University of St Andrews.

Michael Donaghy was born in the Bronx, New York, and now lives in North London. His numerous awards include the Whitbread Prize for Poetry and the Geoffrey Faber Memorial Prize, and he won the Forward Prize for most recent collection, *Conjure* (Picador, 2000). He teaches at City University and Birkbeck College, London, and is a Fellow of the Royal Society of Literature.

Ian Duhig has published three collections of verse with Bloodaxe: *The Bradford Count* (1991), *The Mersey Goldfish* (1995) – shortlisted for the T S Eliot Prize, and *Nominies* (1998) – a Poetry Book Society Special Commendation. He has won the National Poetry Competition on two occasions (1987 and 2001) and was awarded the Forward Prize for Best Poem in 2001.

Aidan Andrew Dun was born in London in 1952, the grandson of the dancer Marie Rambert. He spent his formative years in the West Indies, returned to London in the late '60s and travelled the planet in the following decade. His first epic poem, *Vale Royal*, was published by Goldmark in 1995 and was launched at the Royal Albert Hall. *Universal*, a second epic, has just appeared from the same publisher.

Paul Farley's first collection, *The Boy from the Chemist is Here to See You*, won a Forward Prize and the Somerset Maugham Award, and in 1999 he was the *Sunday Times* Young Writer of the Year. His second book, *The Ice Age* (Picador, 2002), was a Poetry Book Society Choice. He was Writer in Residence at the Wordsworth Trust from 2000-2002 and teaches at Lancaster University.

Peter Finch edited the groundbreaking magazine, *second aeon*, in the '60s and '70s, and was a founder member of Cardiff's Cabaret 246 performance poetry group. His many books include the collections *Antibodies* (Stride, 1997), *Useful* (Seren, 1997), and, most recently, *Food* (Seren, 2002). He currently runs Academi, the Welsh National Literature Promotion Agency.

Jane Griffiths was born in Exeter in 1970 and was brought up in Holland. After reading English at Oxford – where she won the Newdigate Prize – she worked as a bookbinder and as an editor on the *Oxford English Dictionary*. A winner of an Eric Gregory Award in 1996, her first collection, *A Grip on Thin Air*, was published by Bloodaxe in 2000. She is a Lecturer in English at St Edmund Hall, Oxford.

Sophie Hannah is an award-winning poet, novelist and children's writer whose work is studied at GCSE, A-level and degree level. A former Fellow Commoner in Creative Arts at Trinity College, Cambridge, and a Fellow of Wolfson College, Oxford, she now teaches at The Writing School at Manchester Metropolitan University and lives in Bingley, West Yorkshire.

Jane Hill trained at Wimbledon School of Art and has exhibited site-specific work in the UK and abroad, including the Wordsworth Trust, Grasmere. She was Artist in Residence at the Dartington Hall Trust, Devon, during 2000-01, where she produced a narrative installation work for voices.

Ashley Hutchings is a musician and songwriter who is generally considered to be the Father of British Folk-Rock. He founded the three bands which changed the face of folk music in the UK: Fairport Convention, Steeleye Span and The Albion Band. He has also been a music director at the National Theatre and has written and presented programmes on folk-music for the BBC. The first volume of his biography has recently been published by Helter Skelter.

Brendan Kennelly is one of the leading Irish poets of his generation. Born in County Kerry in 1936, he has published more than twenty books of verse, including the controversial *Cromwell* (Beaver Row, Dublin, 1983 & Bloodaxe, 1987) and the best-seller *The Book of Judas* (Bloodaxe, 1991). He has been Professor of Modern Literature at Trinity College, Dublin, since 1973.

Joanna Laurens received great acclaim for her first play, *The Three Birds*, which premiered at London's Gate Theatre and has been performed in Germany and Hungary. Her second play, *Five Gold Rings*, will premiere at London's Almeida Theatre in 2003. She grew up on the Channel Island of Jersey and read English at Queen's University of Belfast, graduating in 2002.

Kona Macphee was born in London and grew up in Melbourne, Australia. She currently lives in Cambridge, where she is a founding director of break-step productions, a digital business consultancy. Her poems have appeared in a number of publications, including *Anvil New Poets 3* and various literary magazines. She received an Eric Gregory Award in 1998.

Jamie McKendrick last collection *Sky Nails* (Faber, 2000) brings together work from his three previous collections, *The Sirocco Room*,

The Kiosk on the Brink and *The Marble Fly* (which won the Forward Prize for Best First Collection in 1997). His next volume, *Ink Stone*, will be published by Faber in January 2003. Jamie McKendrick lives and works in Oxford.

Edwin Morgan was born in Glasgow in 1920 and has spent all but six years of his life in that city. Professor of English at the University until his retirement in 1980, he was named Glasgow's first Poet Laureate in 1999, and, a year later, he was awarded the Queen's Gold Medal for Poetry. His *New Selected Poems*, which were published by Carcanet in 2000, received a Poetry Book Society Recommendation.

Robert Nye was born in London in 1939 and had published poems in the *London Magazine* by the age of 16. He is the author of many volumes of poetry, novels, children's literature, short stories, plays, essays and a libretto. His many prizes include the Eric Gregory Award, The Guardian Fiction Prize and the Hawthornden Prize. He currently lives in Cork, Ireland, and his *Collected Poems* remain in print with Carcanet Press.

Sean O'Brien is a poet, critic, playwright, broadcaster, anthologist and editor. He has won major awards for all five of his collections to date, including the Somerset Maugham Award, the Cholmondeley Award and the E M Forster Award. His latest volume, *Downriver* (Picador, 2001), won the Forward Prize for Best Collection. Poetry critic for *The Sunday Times* and a contributor to both the *Times Literary Supplement* and *The Guardian*, he lives in Newcastle upon Tyne. *Cousin Coat: Selected Poems 1976-2001* is published by Picador in autumn 2002.

Alice Oswald read Classics at Oxford and trained as a gardener with the Royal Horticultural Society at Wisley. Her first collection, *The Thing in the Gap-Stone Stile* (Oxford, 1996) was a Poetry Book Society Choice and was shortlisted for a Forward Prize. Her second volume, *Dart*, was published by Faber in July of this year, and has been named as a PBS Recommendation for Autumn 2002.

Peter Oswald is mostly a verse playwright, whose plays produced include *Fair Ladies at a Game of Poem Cards* (National, 1996), *Augustine's Oak* (The Globe, 1999), *Odysseus* (The Gate, 1999) and *The Ramayana* (Birmingam Rep, 2000). His play *The Golden Ass* is to be staged at the Globe in 2002. All these plays are published by Methuen (*Fair Ladies* . . .) and Oberon books.

Ruth Padel is a Fellow of the Royal Society of Literature and won the 1996 National Poetry Competition. Her recent collections, *Rembrandt Would Have Loved You* and *Voodoo Shop* (Chatto, 1998 & 2002) were Poetry Book Society Choice and Recommendation. Her *52 Ways of Looking at a Poem* (Chatto, 2002) is based on her celebrated newspaper discussion column, 'The Sunday Poem', and contains a lively and informative introduction to reading contemporary poetry.

Jacob Polley is currently working on his debut collection, to be published by Picador in 2003. A Writer in Residence at the Wordsworth Trust, he was awarded the Arts Council of England's 'First Verse' prize in April 2002 and has recently received an Eric Gregory Award from the Society of Authors.

Peter Redgrove has written twenty four volumes of poetry, nine novels and fourteen plays for BBC Radio. His numerous awards include the Guardian Fiction Prize (1973), the Cholmondley Award (1985) and Prix Italia (1982) and in 1996 he was awarded the Queen's Gold Medal for Poetry. He lives with his wife and daughter in Cornwall.

Denise Riley is the author of many books, including *War in the Nursery* (Virago, 1981), *Am I That Name?* (Macmillan, 1988) and *The Words of Selves: Identification, Solidarity, Irony* (Stanford University Press, USA, 2000). Her poetry has been published in several books, including *Penguin Modern Poets 10* with Douglas Oliver and Iain Sinclair, and her *Selected Poems* were brought out by Reality Street Editions in 2000. She lives in London and works at the University of East Anglia.

Penelope Shuttle was born in Middlesex in 1947 and now lives in Cornwall with her husband Peter Redgrove. Her first collection, *The Orchard Upstairs*, was published to great acclaim in 1980 and a further five volumes have appeared. Her most recent book is *A Leaf Out of his Book* (Carcanet / Oxford Poets, 1999).

John Stammers was born in Islington. His first collection, *Panoramic Lounge-Bar* (Picador), is a Poetry Book Society Recommendation, was shortlisted for the Whitbread Poetry Award 2001 and was awarded the Forward/Waterstones Prize for Best First Collection 2001. He is the Judith E Wilson Fellow at the University of Cambridge from October 2002.

Greta Stoddart was born in Henley-on-Thames in 1966 and grew up in Belgium and Oxford. Her debut volume, *At Home in the Dark* (Anvil, 2001), was shortlisted for the Forward Prize for Best First Collection and won the Geoffrey Faber Memorial Prize 2002. She is currently Poetry Tutor at Morley College in London and Visiting Fellow at Warwick University.

Paul Stubbs was born in Norwich and has had his work published in several literary magazines. He has written a version of Euripides' *Bacchae* and is currently working on a version of Dante's *Paradiso*.

Charles Tomlinson was born in Stoke-on-Trent in 1927. He studied at Cambridge and taught at the University of Bristol from 1957 until his retirement. He has published many volumes of poetry, including a *Selected Poems* (Carcanet, 1997), as well as works of criticism and translation. He also edited the *Oxford Book of Verse in English Translation* (1980).

Sarah Wardle won the Geoffrey Dearmer Prize, *Poetry Review*'s New Poet of the Year Award, in 1999. She has had poems and reviews in *Poetry Review*, *PN Review*, *London Magazine*, the *TLS* and *The Observer*. A selection appeared in *Anvil New Poets 3* (Anvil 2001). Her first collection is forthcoming from Bloodaxe.